THE WORK
OF THE
HOLY
SPIRIT

THE WORK
OF THE
HOLY
SPIRIT

Jessie Penn-Lewis

CLC PUBLICATIONS

Fort Washington, PA 19034

The Work of the Holy Spirit
Published by CLC Publications

U.S.A.
P.O. Box 1449, Fort Washington, PA 19034

UNITED KINGDOM
CLC International (UK)
Unit 5, Glendale Avenue, Sandycroft, Flintshire, CH5 2QP

Originally published by Overcomer Literature Trust, England
First American edition 1992
This printing 2017

Printed in the United States of America

ISBN (paperback): 978-0-87508-961-4

Unless otherwise noted, Scripture quotations are from the
Holy Bible, King James Version, 1611.

Scripture quotations marked ASV are from the Holy Bible,
American Standard Version, 1901.

Italics in Scripture quotations are the emphasis of the author.

Contents

Chapter 1

The Comforter

*The Gift of the Comforter—The Spirit of Truth—
The Way to Know Him—He Shall Be in You—
The Day They Would Know—The Gethsemane Agony*

IT is of supreme importance in seeking to understand spiritual things that we recognize the Holy Spirit as the Revealer of the things of God. Let us turn to the Lord's last farewell to His disciples in John 14:16–17. "*I will pray the Father, and He shall give you another Comforter, that He may abide with you for ever, even the Spirit of truth, whom the world cannot receive.*" These are the actual words which the Lord Jesus Christ spoke from His own lips the night before He was betrayed and crucified.

You know how you treasure the words of those you love—some tender friend or relative

who has died; how you go back to the last words
that one spoke. Here we have the Lord Jesus
speaking with His twelve disciples around Him.
No! The little circle of twelve was now broken,
and there were only eleven! *Judas' place was empty!*
There had been twelve, but one of the company
had gone out to betray his Master, and while
the Lord Jesus was talking words of heavenly
tenderness to the faithful eleven, Judas was outside betraying Him!

Even though He knew this, the heart of the
Lord Jesus was at leisure and in such a calm rest
of God that there was not a trace of unrest about
Him. There He sat, in perfect peace, just giving
His last words to this little company.

The Gift of the Comforter

Jesus said to them so tenderly, "I will pray
the Father, and He shall give you another Comforter." Take these words into your heart and
ask that He may be made known to you. It is
good to have mental knowledge, but such knowledge does not satisfy the heart. The greatest thing
that is needed in the world today is the personal
knowledge of a Comforter who will make known

the unseen Saviour. "He shall give you another Comforter, that He may abide with you"—for I am going away, but I will send you Someone who will abide with you forever, "even the Spirit of Truth."

The Spirit of Truth

This is His own special name. He is the Spirit of Truth. He always tells you the truth. But He is One "whom the world cannot receive." Poor world! Poor world! It cannot receive the Comforter! Poor empty world; there is no "comfort" for the world unless it will turn to God. There is only judgment for the world!

Poor people of the world—they have no comfort! They are without any anchor to hold them in the storms of life. They have hearts, as God's children have, and they have troubles . . . but they are without comfort. They can be happy in the theater and in all sorts of ways when days are bright; but when they come to the stern facts of life, they are without comfort. Poor world! "The world cannot receive [Him] because it seeth Him not, neither knoweth Him; but ye know Him for He dwelleth with you and shall be in you."

"*Ye know Him!*" Do you? Do you know the Comforter? Or are you just like the world when you are in trouble? Do you know the Holy Spirit? Or do you simply know a historical Christ, and that the Holy Spirit was given on the Day of Pentecost? Do you think of Him as an "influence" or speak of Him as "it"? The Lord Jesus says "He" and "Him" because He is a person. Do you know Him, the Person?

The historical faith in Christ is of little comfort. There are numbers of people who profess to be Christians but do not know Christ. They have opinions, ideas, theories and even theologies, but they do not know Him. So I ask you again, do you know Him?

Do you know the living Christ? If not, it means that you do not know the Holy Spirit, for He reveals the living Christ—that is, His work. Do you know? Or do you say, I think, I believe, I hope, I have this view, this opinion?

The Way to Know Him

"Ye know Him!" How? "He *dwelleth* with you." That is how you get to know people. Putting it in a very rough, earthly way, that is how

He is known. "He dwelleth with you; and He shall be in you!" You know Him by experience, not by theory, nor by a mental knowledge. Anything you know in that way can soon be stripped away from you; but something that you have proved, and you know from experience, no human being in this world can take from you.

This is how the martyrs lived through their sufferings. God puts a living faith and knowledge of Himself into His people, something which not even martyrdom can tear out of them. Martyrdom may take away opinions from men, and views and ideas, but no martyrdom can take out of the fiber of one's being what is wrought into it through personal knowledge and experience.

That, I say, is what God wants to do for us. He wants the Holy Spirit to be a real Person in us to make Christ real to us in life, so that we cannot help living in the Living One. It is not what you believe or think, but it is what you are—what is wrought into you as part of you, and what is greater than all you merely see. "Ye know Him, for He shall be in you."

He Shall Be In You

There is a wonderful gleam of light in Dr. Elder Cummings' book on the Holy Spirit about that sentence "He shall be in you." He says that it means the Holy Spirit entering in and clothing Himself with you just as He did with Gideon. Your outer body becomes a clothing, to embody, so to speak, the Holy Spirit dwelling in the inner shrine of your spirit.

The Holy Spirit wants to reach the people, but He is Spirit and they are flesh; and how can flesh be reached by Spirit? There is no way of contact between them. Hence the poor world goes on its way, with its theories and views, and without knowledge of God. We might almost erect an altar in Christendom, such as Paul saw in Athens, "To the unknown God." They know about Him, but the majority do not know Him.

But the Holy Spirit wants to enter and to clothe Himself with you, as an outer garment made for Him, that through your thoughts and through your lives He may work and reach the world. "He shall clothe Himself with you" as "the Spirit of the Lord clothed Himself with Gideon," so that a weak, trembling Gideon went forth in the might of God, and all Israel was gathered after him.

Dear listeners, are your hearts now saying, "Oh God, make me know Him"? I do not want to meet your intellects, nor your feelings, nor your views. I desire to disentangle you from all these and just say to you, "Do you know the Holy Spirit? And, by the Holy Spirit, do you know the Lord Jesus Christ, and do you know the Father? Do you *know* God?"

The Day They Would Know

Our Lord proceeds in His talk with His disciples, saying, "At that day ye shall know." He spoke about a day. What day? Why, the day when He would pray the Father, and He would give the other Comforter. That day could not come until Christ had gone to the cross, to the tomb and through the tomb had gone back to the Father. That day was to come then.

While speaking to them He was on the eve of the cross, and yet He was speaking as though He was going to be alive. Think of one on the edge of death, talking about going to the Father to receive the Comforter for His orphaned disciples. How little there would be in all that He was saying if He was not going to rise again.

"At that day I will pray the Father, and He will give you another Comforter," and that day in its manifestations was the Day of Pentecost. Between the day He was speaking these words and the day of the Holy Spirit's coming, the Lord Jesus was to go to the cross. Oh, what lay between these words and that day! After speaking thus to them, He went out to the garden of Gethsemane, to such an agony as could not long have continued unabated.

The Gethsemane Agony

We are told by the writer to the Hebrews that with strong crying and tears Christ prayed to God to save Him out of death, in that anguish in Gethsemane; for had He died in Gethsemane, the world would not have been redeemed, and the Holy Spirit would not have been given. If His body had given way under the anguish of the Garden passion, He would not have reached the cross. An angel was sent from heaven to Him in that agony to strengthen His body to endure the anguish and to enable

Him to bear all that was coming upon Him in that path from Gethsemane to Calvary.

In that path to the cross after the anguish of the Garden, do you realize that the Lord Jesus walked seven miles that awful night, from Pilate to Herod and back, from one person to another, beaten by the soldiers and scoffed at by the mob? Seven weary miles He traveled, in patience that never uttered a murmur, that never said, "I cannot bear it," and that never for one minute turned around on His tormentors. He was the *perfect man*!

And it was by the Holy Spirit, who is God, that He was strengthened to endure it. Step by step He went to that cross, and there on Calvary for the atonement of the world's sin He died for you and for me. Now we can say, "He bore my sin in His own body on the tree" (1 Pet. 2:24); yes, your sins and mine.

Chapter 2

The Revealer
of the Things of God

*God Manifest in the Flesh—The Holy Spirit
the Teacher—The Holy Spirit Bears Witness to Christ*

THOSE who followed Christ to Calvary, and
those who saw Him die, came to understand that His death meant atonement, redemp-
tion and salvation. To these He had said, "I will
pray the Father, and He shall give you another
Comforter." Ye shall have *comfort*. You shall not
see simply a tragedy—the bruised body and the
flowing blood—but you shall see the *glory* of
the cross.

The world will see the outward agony, and
the patience and beauty of the dying Lamb, and
the world will say, "Never was there a man who

suffered like that!" But you shall have the Comforter, and through Him you shall know that by that sacrifice you are redeemed. You shall realize the blotting out of your sins *through that blood* and the comfort through that blood of the clear open vision of God. As if the Lord had said, "You shall not merely see Me on the cross but you shall see Me one with the Father in heaven; you shall know that I am God, and came from God; for in that day ye shall know that I am in the Father" (see John 14:20).

God Manifest in the Flesh

What man, who was *only man*, would talk like this on the eve of an awful death upon a gallows? No, "*this* man" was "God manifest in the flesh" (1 Tim. 3:16).

Now let me ask you: What have you done with all these wonderful words? Is it all written in the Scriptures and yet you have failed to realize their encouragement? Have you said, "Jesus said that to His disciples, but not to me"? No, He said it to you, to you. Then what are you going to do?

He said, "I will give you another Comforter." Let me ask you again: If you have received the

Holy Spirit, have these things become real to you by the Holy Spirit? Is the Lord Jesus Christ *really* God to you? Do you know the ascended Christ on the throne? Do you know that you are joined with Him in His risen life? Do you *know* that "your life is hid with Christ in God" (Col. 3:3)?

He is still the same Jesus. He told His disciples before He died, "*At that day ye shall know that I am in My Father, and ye in Me, and I in you.*" The very same Christ came to the Apostle Paul and revealed His gospel to him, and the meaning of the cross (Gal. 1:11–12). "*Ye are dead, and your life is hid with Christ in God*" (Col. 3:3). That is your position now if you are His child. You are joined to the risen Christ, and your place is with Him in the Father's presence. He is to be your life now on the earth.

"Christ who is our life" (Col. 3:4). "The riches of the glory of this mystery . . . which is Christ in you the hope of glory" (Col. 1:27). "I have been crucified with Christ; and it is no longer I that live, but Christ liveth in me: and that life which I now live in the flesh I live in faith which is in the Son of God, who loved me and gave Himself up for me" (Gal. 2:20, ASV). It is all one message, and the Holy Spirit is the One who makes it real to us.

If any man say, "Oh, this is not for me; this is too great for me," remember the Master said, "Thou hast bid these things from the wise and prudent, and hast revealed them unto babes" (Matt. 11:25)! "Except ye . . . become as little children, ye shall not enter into the Kingdom" (Matt. 18:3). Come as a little child and say, "Oh, blessed Spirit, show me these things, and open them to me; make them real to me, cause me to understand them, and I will receive them."

Now let us think about the Holy Spirit and His work in connection with the cross, and let us turn again to John 14:16: "I will pray the Father, and He shall give you another Comforter . . . whom the world cannot receive, because it seeth Him not, neither knoweth Him."

The world always wants something it can see, something material and tangible. We cannot see the air, and yet we know it is there by its effects. There are many such unseen things that are known by their visible effects, such as the law of gravitation. Although knowing these things, the world is entirely illogical when it comes to spiritual things. It wants to see before it can believe.

The Lord Jesus was on the eve of the cross. It was the night before He went to Calvary. He was opening His heart to His disciples. He knew how they would feel when He had gone from them, so He said to them, "I will pray the Father, and He shall give you another Comforter."

The Holy Spirit was given by the Father in answer to the request of the Lord Jesus, for a definite purpose. Jesus went back to the glory and sat down at the night hand of the Father. He sent the Holy Spirit to take His place in the world, to dwell in His redeemed ones; so He calls Him "*another* Comforter." The very first work the Holy Spirit does is expressed in His name "the Comforter." He does not drive or whip human beings, because He has come to *comfort* them as He dwells in the heart.

In verse 26 of the fourteenth of John we read: "The Comforter, even the Holy Spirit, whom the Father will send in My name" (ASV). First, it is "whom the Father will *give*" (v. 16); then "whom the Father will *send* in My name." He is sent because the Lord asked for Him, and when He is sent it is "in His name."

Coming as He does in the name of the Lord Jesus, it is said that the Holy Spirit "shall teach you all things." The scope of His teaching is stated in the words: "All that *I said* unto you." He was to bring back to them the words of Christ, because they did not understand them when they were first spoken (John 12:16). They understood them as little as we do at first. When the Lord Jesus talked to them about heavenly things, they thought of earthly things—just as we do.

The Holy Spirit the Teacher

All things that the Lord said to His disciples when on earth, the Holy Spirit was to take and, as a Teacher, *explain them and make the hearers understand their meaning.* He is the teacher to-day also of all who are willing to be taught by Him about the words of Christ. We can understand what is said about the Lord Jesus in this Book only by the illuminating of the Holy Spirit. "*He shall teach you.*"

Have you ever knelt down and asked the Holy Spirit to teach you? Or do you think you can find out these things for yourself? But it says plainly: "The *natural* man receiveth not the things of the Spirit of God . . . because they are spiritually discerned."[1] You may even have the life of the Lord Jesus in you, and yet the "natural man" in you may be trying to understand the things of God. It cannot. Paul says, "We have received, not the spirit of the world, but the Spirit which is of God; that we might know the things that are freely given to us by God" (1 Cor. 2:12). If you recognize the complete inability of the "natural man"—your *natural* capacity—to understand, or to discern, or to perceive the things of God, then you may be taught by the Spirit of God. The "man of soul," that is, the man of intellect, cannot receive the things of God; for they are spiritually discerned.

"Now we have received the Spirit which is of God," said the great man of intellect, the Apostle Paul. There has not been an intellect, either in that day or this, greater than that of the Apostle Paul. Yet Paul preached a crucified Christ and wrote as he did of the unseen things: "The natural man"—the man of soul—"cannot receive the things of the Spirit, for they are spiritually discerned."

When reading your Bible, and in fact every

---

1. See and read carefully 1 Corinthians 2:14, and note the marginal readings.

other book giving spiritual truth, acknowledge your need of the Holy Spirit as the Teacher, and ask Him to enable you to know the "things" which are "freely given you by God." You cannot have these "things" as your own possession unless you know them. You may be heir to one hundred thousand dollars, but if you do not know it you are no richer.

So the Holy Spirit has come that we may *know* the things that are given to us. You don't have to beg for them; you have only to *know* that they are given you, for the Holy Spirit's work is to show you all the things which are freely given to you by God, and given only that you may take them. The Lord Jesus said this plainly. Therefore you want not only *comfort*, but you want *knowledge*. You need to know what your possessions are in Christ so as to get the comfort of them, and the Holy Spirit is your teacher.

The Holy Spirit Bears Witness to Christ

Here too is another wonderful part of our Lord's promise: He said, "*When* the Comforter is come." Well, He has come; He came at Pentecost—"whom I will send unto you from the

Father, even the Spirit of truth, which proceedeth from the Father, He shall bear witness of Me" (John 15:26, ASV). Not only the Holy Spirit to explain, to illuminate, to make real to you the words of Christ; but to "bear witness" of Christ—what He *did*, what He *is*, what He *will do* in "things that are to come."[2]

In brief, His whole work is *to testify of the Lord Jesus*: Christ on Calvary; Christ in the grave; Christ raised from the grave; received up into glory, and "made to sit" at the right hand of God; then receiving from the Father the gift of the Holy Spirit, and sending Him down to earth to make Him as real to you in your life as the Man the disciples knew and talked to; to make Him known to you here and now (John 14:18–20).

When you are speaking to the Lord Jesus in prayer and fellowship, remember it is actually as real "in the Spirit" as it was for the disciples when speaking to Him. He is the very same Jesus whom Peter addressed. Yes, the very same. Two thousand years are nothing to God! You can speak to the Lord Jesus Christ now as He is in His glorified body—that same Person to whom Peter spoke that morning on the seashore when

---

2. See John 16:13–14.

He spread the fish for them to eat. You can have actual fellowship with the same Lord they knew then. The very same Lord Jesus will answer you by His Spirit *in your spirit* and through His Word.[3]

---

3. See Hebrews 13:8, Acts 1:11, Revelation 1:12–18.

Chapter 3

The Meaning of Calvary

Why Did Jesus Die?—The Second Aspect of Calvary—
The Supply of the Spirit of Jesus—"No Longer I"

WHEN He, the Spirit of Truth, is come, "He shall testify of Me" (John 15:26). The very first witness of the Spirit is to the Lord Jesus as the Crucified One on the cross.

First, that the Lord Jesus, the Son of God, hanging upon that cross bore the sins of the world upon Himself. "He shall bear witness of Me" (ASV). He bears witness to the crucified Christ, and then to the ascended and exalted Christ and all that He is in the glory.

The Holy Spirit makes the fact of Christ's death as real to you as if you had stood with the disciples at the foot of the cross. He will take you over the two thousand years and make that place called "a skull," outside the city walls of Jerusalem, as real to you in your spirit as it was to the eyes of the ones who stood there. Martin Luther said, "I feel as if Jesus Christ died but yesterday!"

Why Did Jesus Die?

Why did the Lord Jesus die? Peter says, "He bore our sins in His own body on the tree" (1 Pet. 2:24). You cannot possibly get anything plainer than that. There is no getting away from its meaning. You may change one word in the statement and say, "He bore my sins in His own body on the tree." That is why Paul said that He "made peace through the blood of His cross" (Col. 1:20). Seven hundred years before Christ came, the prophet Isaiah said, "The Lord hath laid on Him the iniquity of us all" (Isa. 53:6).

Unless you know you are a sinner, you do not *want* a Saviour. The knowledge that you are a captive to sin leads to the desire for a Deliverer. Christ came "not to call the righteous, but sinners to repentance." It is only when the Holy Spirit shows you what sin is that you want a Saviour. Then you go to the statement so eagerly,

"Him who knew no sin He *made to be sin on our behalf*; that we might become the righteousness of God in Him" (2 Cor. 5:21, ASV).

Those who carry God's message are deeply conscious that when men are speaking such words as these, none of the persons who listen can understand what they mean apart from the Holy Spirit. A short time ago in an evangelistic campaign, the Spirit of God was working so mightily that it could be seen how He applied the word.

The speaker at the time was talking about sin and Calvary, when a woman sitting in the furthermost end of the gallery cried aloud with a piercing cry, across the mass of people, "*You are speaking about me. What you are saying is true.* I am a sinner; I am a sinner, God have mercy upon me!" She fell upon her knees, while the awe upon the people was so deep that they did not even turn to look at the one who cried. It seemed as though the speaker and the woman were the only people in the Hall.

That is what the Holy Spirit does! He convicts of sin. "*You are speaking about me; I am a sinner!*" she said. When you are thus convicted of sin, you want a Saviour who bore your sins in

His own body on the tree. It is because your sins were nailed to the cross in the person of Christ that God can forgive you and blot them out.

The blood of Jesus Christ does blot out sin. If you have fallen into the deepest, blackest sin, only the blood of Jesus Christ can remove it. This is what the Holy Spirit bears witness to, and there are thousands of souls who bear co-witness with the Holy Spirit that the blood of Jesus has washed away sin. A witness to such a fact is more effective than any mere teaching of the Atonement. If all the "theories" of the Atonement today were torn to shreds, you could not destroy the personal witness of millions to Calvary's power.

The Second Aspect of Calvary

Let us now note the second aspect of Calvary, as stated in Romans 6:6: "*Our old man was crucified with Him*" (ASV). When Christ was hanging on that cross on Calvary's hill, "our old man"—our old self, the old "creation"—was crucified with Him. Paul says the gospel he preached *was revealed to him by the risen Christ Himself* (Gal. 1:12). It is one thing to have your sins blotted out; it is another thing to be delivered from their *power* so that you are not under their mastery. You may get rid of the *guilt* of sin, the *burden* of sin, without understanding how to get the victory over the *power* of sin.

You may have a secret besetting sin, and you try your very utmost to conquer it, saying, "I will not do it." But alas, you do it again. Sin as a master is too strong for you. The only way to get free from that master is to die to him.[1] There is then the severance and the freedom which comes through death. Death frees even the slave from the tyranny of his master.

So also the way of *victory over* and *freedom from* sin is not only to believe that the Lord Jesus Christ bore our sins on the cross and that God will, on that account, forgive them when you confess them (1 John 1:9); you must also understand that *you yourself died with Jesus Christ on that cross*, and now you can *reckon* you are *dead to sin*. That is to say, you take this attitude to sin: "I have died to you, you have no claim on me. The Lord Jesus took me to His cross, and I stand in a position of death to the old life,

---

1. Read over and over the whole chapter of Romans 6, asking the Holy Spirit to make you understand it.

to the old habits, to the old ways, to the old plans."

When you do this, and put your will to this decision and position, the Holy Spirit works on the ground of the death of Christ and places a real gulf of *death* between you and the old things. It is just as if you yourself were on Calvary's cross, looking at your old life with a gulf of death between you and it. This is made real to you by the Holy Spirit as you stand in that attitude of faith in your identification with Christ as declared in God's Word.

The Supply of the Spirit of Jesus

As soon as you appropriate the fact that you have died with Christ—that the old life is crucified—and you hold that attitude moment by moment, the Holy Spirit communicates to you *the very life of Christ moment by moment.* He gives you a supply of the Spirit of Jesus (Phil. 1:19), and thus you can be, by His power, what you could not be otherwise apart from Christ.

He gives you divine strength in your weakness. He gives you power to triumph over the things that once defeated you, and *He imparts to you the very life* that is now in the Lord Jesus in glory. "He that hath the Son hath *the life*" (1 John 5:12, ASV). "When Christ, *who is our life*, shall appear, then shall ye also appear with Him in glory" (Col. 3:4). "Christ in you, the hope of glory" (Col. 1:27).

We have seen that the Holy Spirit is charged with the work of testifying to Christ, and this means testifying to *every aspect of His finished redemptive work* on Calvary. When He has revealed the Lord Jesus as Saviour, then His great work is to bring to death in actuality the "old creation," to make room for the life of Christ in the believer so that he grows up into Him (Eph. 4:15) into full growth.

The Holy Spirit must bring the old creation, that is to say, the old life in you, to the place of death so that He may put in the life of Christ. The old creature-life must be broken and put to death to make room for the new life in the center of the being to grow—a life that has eternal power in it. If you are a child of God, there is locked up in you—in the very center of your being, in your spirit—a divine power and a divine life. But possibly it cannot get out because it is covered over by the outside things, until those around you would never think that you really loved the Lord at all.

Your deep need is to understand the meaning of the cross, which shows that the Lord Jesus not only carried on to that cross your *sins* but that He took *you* there with Him!

When the Roman Christians were debating whether they ought to continue in sin or not, Paul said, "How shall we, that are dead to sin, live any longer therein?" How *can* you live in a thing you have died to? Supposing you had actually died to this world, how could you live in it? And if you have died to *sin*, how can you go on living under *its* power?

"No Longer I"

In Galatians 2:20 (ASV) Paul says, "I have been crucified with Christ; and it is no longer I that live, but Christ liveth in me: and that life which I now live in the flesh I live in faith, the faith which is in the Son of God, who loved me, and gave Himself up for me." Have you ever caught sight of that meaning of the cross? Have you ever been to the foot of Calvary and seen hanging on that cross not only the Lord Jesus

Christ but yourself? Yourself in Him.

In the Greek of Galatlans 2:20, there is another word which has not been brought out in the English. "I have been crucified *together* with Christ." "God forbid that I should glory, save in the cross of our Lord Jesus Christ, by whom the world is crucified unto me, and I unto the world" (Galatians 6:14).

How does this work? It simply means that when you take the position of the old life crucified, the new life has room in you to grow. God becomes a reality to you; and you, although in the world, instead of being conformed to it, become crucified to the world by the cross of the Lord Jesus Christ. This is the only true way to have victory over sin.

It is not saying "I will not get into a temper," but it is quietly and deliberately taking your position with Christ at Calvary and saying, "Lord Jesus, I have died to that temper, on the cross with Thee. I count upon the Holy Spirit to separate me from it, for I have died to it. I cannot manage it; it is beyond me. But I have died to it." In the center of your will you take "an attitude" of death and say, "I have nothing to do with it; I refuse it *because* I have died with

Christ."

The law of faith is in this attitude, which, if put into operation by the act or the reckoning of your will, opens a path between you and the risen Lord for His life-power to flow into your whole being. That is reckoning yourself dead indeed unto sin, and reckoning yourself alive unto God.

Chapter 4

Victory the Ideal

*The Mind Open to the Holy Spirit—
The Walk in Victory*

WE have talked together of the victory over sin explained in Romans 6. Now in the same way we need to learn the way of victory over Satan. When you take the position that you have died with Christ to sin, and reckon it as fact *now*, the devil begins to attack you through his wicked spirits. He knows that, in union with Christ, Calvary is victory to the Christian. If this position in Christ is taken, he can do nothing; for *the cross is the one place where he is powerless.*

If you say when the enemy tempts, "I have died on the cross with Christ; I have nothing to do with you . . ." you will find victory over Satan, as well as over sin.

It also means victory over wandering thoughts. When you take the position of victory—death with Christ to sin— then it works into all the different parts of your being. It may be impatience, or temper, or a crooked disposition. It may be a particular department of the mind. Satan pours all kinds of thoughts through your mind.

Why do you allow this? Are you troubled when you kneel to pray, so that you cannot keep your mind on what you pray? Do awful blasphemous thoughts pass through your mind when you seek to worship or pray? Are you tortured with things presented to your mind that you hate? Does the devil keep you crushed with them, saying, "If you were a Christian you would not have these thoughts"?

Just answer, "No, it is not I; I have died, it is not I. I will not take your lies. I will have nothing to do with you." By the choice of your will based on the victory death and life of Christ you can shut the door of your mind to Satan.

The Mind Open to the Holy Spirit

If your mind were closed to all the things

that Satan sends, it would be open to the Holy Spirit to pour into it all the blessed truths of God. The reason why God's people listen to and read the Bible so much and yet the truth remains sealed for them is simply because the mind is not purified by the Holy Spirit of God. They have asked for "new hearts," but not for "new heads."

A great many of the divisions between God's children do not come from the heart but from the *head*! It is through the mind that *jealousy*, for example, comes—a little thought being put into the mind by Satan, which the person admits; and then in the light of that jealous thought the other person is seen. From whence does it come? Not necessarily from the heart, but from the head.

If only God's children understood this one simple position of "I died" and then refused to let Satan have an entrance to any part of their being. If they would close the door to him when he brings his charges against them, by saying, "Is that my choice? No, it does not belong to me; it is what the enemy is pouring on me, and I refuse to take it in. I have died with Christ"— then they would realize the path of victory.

Set your minds to know victory—victory of heart, victory of mind, victory over impatience, victory over sin, victory over Satan. If all Christians knew this personal victory God would have an army to send out against the devil.

Christians are unable to win souls because they themselves have no personal victory. They are ashamed of themselves in their hearts. They say, "How can I go to speak for Christ? Have I not secret sin holding me down?" This is often why they cannot pray in prayer meetings.

Have you personal victory in every part of your life? If you had, the Holy Spirit could then begin to work through you. You could not keep silent when meeting with others to pray. Think of people in the slums, the drunkards in bonds, the slaves to sin on every hand and the feeble church in the midst of them. What is the matter? Is it not lack of *personal victory*? With personal victory there is a readiness to go out to reach others.

The Walk In Victory

As you thus walk in victory, you learn to know the equipping by the Holy Spirit for service. The Holy Spirit does not equip for service before He makes you personally victorious over sin; so your victory is very important to the whole army of the Lord. If you live in victory in your home when things go wrong, and do not get crushed when the devil comes to drive and discourage you, then you will know what power is. Others will come to you and ask you what has happened, and solicit your help. How quickly there would be revival if all God's children knew how to live a victorious life!

There are two kinds of service which follow this equipping by the Holy Spirit: one a service of helping others and another kind of service which we might call "conflict service," meaning not only war on sin, but *war on Satan*. When the Holy Spirit has wrought into you the meaning of the cross and led you to take your position of saying "I have died," and worked it into you in practical life, then you can ask the Holy Spirit to clothe you for aggressive service. He will give you aggressive power so that you can not only go out in victory for others, in speech, testimony and *prayer*, but also have power to attack the kingdom of Satan, as one nation goes to war on another in the world sphere.

There is a great war going on in the unseen sphere. The powers of darkness are at work all around us. You cannot fight them with carnal weapons. The weapon of prayer is the effective weapon. What is needed for the church just now is not only an army of speakers to witness to Christ but *an army of those who can pray*; those who know how to be in prayer as a meeting proceeds, binding the devil from interfering with the message given.

Often those who know the Holy Spirit, and go forward to testify for Him, have to say, "Alas, what is the matter?" The people perhaps are blamed for their hardness, or the workers blame themselves. They say, "I *did* know the fullness of the Holy Spirit, yet the ground is very hard in this place." Although they may have received the Holy Spirit in power, unless they have some intercessors who know how to pray that hardness away, they cannot reach the people with power.

The Holy Spirit gives to some aggressive power to witness for Christ, but He also gives to others *aggressive power to pray*; and the two must work together.

Pray that God will teach you and put you in a position of victory where you can effectively say, "Oh Lord, bind the devil" (See Matt. 12:29). Thus you will learn victory in union with Christ. We need to learn how to appropriate and apply the victory of Calvary, and prove that Satan was conquered at the cross of Christ. (See John 12:31.)

Chapter 5

The Law of Life
in the Inward Man

The Law of the Spirit of Life–The Decision of the Will–
Co-operation With the Spirit of Life–
The Need of Watching

IN Romans 8:2 we read, "The law of the Spirit of life in Christ Jesus hath made me free from the law of sin and death"; and in chapter 7:23, "I see another law in my members, warring against the law of my mind, and bringing me into captivity to the law of sin which is in my members." In Romans 7:22 we read, "For I delight in the law of God after the *inward man*." It is written in Ephesians 3:16, "Strengthened with might by His Spirit in the *inner man*." What is the "inward man" referred to here? Bishop Moule says that this "inward man," in Ephesians 3:16, means the regenerate human spirit; so we might read it, "strengthened with might by the Holy Spirit in our human spirit"—the "inward man."

"I delight in the will of God," or the law of God, "in the *inward man*," writes the apostle in Romans 7:22. The "inward man" is right-intended, but—this is a big "but"—"I see another law in *my members*." What are the members? Hands, feet, the outer case of the human body. "I see another law in *my members*, warring against the law of my mind, and bringing me into captivity to the law of sin which is in my members."

Let us read it quite simply like this, "I see a law in my *body*, causing it to fight against the inward man in my center." The body is such a weight. Oh, we cry, if my "members" were only liberated to do the will of God! If my "members" were only free! Let us, for instance, take the tongue. Oh, if this tongue would not say what it does. If it were only kept in the peace of God in which I delight in the center of my being! Who shall deliver me from the body of this death?

The Law of the Spirit of Life

Read the answer to this cry: "The law of the *Spirit of life* in Christ Jesus hath made me free from the law of sin and death" (Rom. 8:2). What the full meaning of this text is we cannot now explain. But there is a practical message in it for us, which we may briefly summarize as the promise of the Spirit of life so dwelling in the spirit as to keep us in a place of freedom from the "law" which is in the body, dragging us down.

And not only the law of *sin* in the body, but *the law of death*—the death in our bodies always at work—may be rendered inoperative moment by moment, by the Spirit of life, as we abide in Christ our risen Lord. You are to live according to the "Spirit of life" in your spirit. As you obey and cooperate with that law, you will be kept free from the working of that other law which is dragging you down day by day. "The law of the Spirit of life in Christ Jesus hath *made me free* from the law of sin and death."

The result of this obedience and cooperation with the Spirit of life you will find in Romans 8:4 (ASV, margin): "That the requirement of the law"—*i.e.*, the commandments or will of God—"might be fulfilled in us, who walk not after the flesh, but after the Spirit." Here we have reference to a "walk." To walk means action, and a walk can only be step by step.

How do you walk? According to this verse there is "somebody" at the center who decides *how* to walk. There is the "inward" man at the center who decides moment by moment—step by step—whether the outer man shall "walk" after the flesh, which is the lower sphere, or "after the Spirit," which is the higher sphere. Hour by hour the "inward man" decides. (See v. 5.)

The Decision of the Will

This momentary *decision* of the "center" as to how the outer man shall walk is of great importance. You must *decide* what you will do— whether you will walk according to the higher or the lower part of your being.

And you need not now say you "cannot help" your body ruling, because "the law of the Spirit of life" can liberate you from being mastered by the "law" in its members—that law of sin, and that law of death. There is death in your body, causing powerlessness and weight, but there is also in your spirit the Spirit of life, with another power or "law" which, if you will obey, will give you liberty to walk after the law of God with ease and joy.

We children of God must learn this for the conflict of today; for if we live in the lower sphere in any degree whatsoever, we shall give advantage to the power of the enemy. Nothing else than living according to the "Spirit of life" in the inward man will keep us free from being dragged down under the power of sin or death, and enable us instead to walk in victory.

Let us emphasize again that it is a moment-by-moment "walk." They that *walk* after the flesh do *mind* the things of the flesh. Here we have the feet guided by the mind, "walking" in accord with the knowledge and decisions of the mind. The opposite is also true: They that *walk* after the Spirit do *mind* the things of the Spirit.

Which do you "mind" all day long? These two spheres come before you clearly, and *you* are to have a choice all day long which you will do. Are you minding the things of the flesh? Are you caring about them? Are you listening to them, and giving your mind to them?

Or are you minding the things of the Spirit? Are you most concerned to live by the Spirit?

Are you depending upon the "Spirit of life" to give you clear vision? Are you asking the Holy Spirit to shed light upon your path, so that you can tell which path you are walking in? "The law of the Spirit of life in Christ Jesus" keeps us from being dominated by that law of sin and death. "After the Spirit," not "after the flesh."

Paul says the fruit of obeying the flesh is *death*. He also says that the "mind of the flesh" is enmity against God, but the mind of the Spirit is "life and peace." If you walk after the Spirit—the higher power—you have life and peace. If you obey the lower law, it means "enmity"—*i.e.*, a "fight" against God—and "death," *i.e.*, powerlessness.

Cooperation with the Spirit of Life

Do you understand that cooperation with the Spirit of life in Christ makes your body respond to the "law of the Spirit?" The body is not then, as it were, a "dead weight." It is not then a carrying about, so to speak, of a "body of death."

But shall we not always have this "body of death"? Shall we not be subject still to the law of death? Yes, but the law of the Spirit of life will enable you to live above it. You, through your will in the center of the outward man, must choose. If you obey the "body" and listen to its cries and groanings, you will go under it. But the "law of the Spirit of life" in your inward man—in your spirit—can keep you free from being controlled by the law working in the body, for it is made inoperative while you walk according to the Spirit.

What must I do, you ask? Simply this: Say, "I recognize the Spirit of life in my spirit, and I count upon the Spirit of life to set me free from being dragged down by the lower law, either of sin or of death."

Have you ever thought that it is possible for you to be kept in triumph above the law of death? You know that "death works" in your body all the time, and that it is only kept alive by your continual breathing. It is a "dying body"—dying every minute. It is only being kept alive by air, food and rest. Without these outer supplies it would die.

Speaking according to physical laws, God gives *you* a controlling—a mastering—power over the death in your body, as you take the supply of both air and food which you need. And in analogy, Paul goes on to say, "The body is *dead* because of sin; but the spirit is *life* because of righteousness" (Rom. 8:10, ASV). Righteousness, imputed and imparted, comes in here.

The "Spirit of life" works only as you are in accord with the God of righteousness. If your life is wrong, and you do that which is not right, you will be subject to the law of death immediately. Yes, even if you know how to live by the Spirit of life, if you do wrong, you will quickly become subject to the law of sin and death.

How can you then get back to the life-plane? First of all, you must ask the Lord to deal with the lapse into the lower plane as *sin* and to pardon and cleanse you by His blood (1 John 1:9). Then ask the Holy Spirit to show you if anything contrary to what is *right* in God's sight has come in, and then put the thing right. You obey the lower, and you go down under its "law"—you obey the higher, and you go back to the higher plane of life according to its law. "If we live by the Spirit, by the Spirit let us also walk" (Galatians 5:25, ASV).

Do you understand that an unkind word about anybody is according to the lower law—

the law of sin and death? To live according to the Spirit will compel you to examine every step you take. You will learn to say about a certain thing, "Is it according to the mind of the Spirit?" You say "No!" Well, *what is it, then*? You must *define what it is.*

There is no neutral ground here. Every step you take is "after the flesh" or "after the Spirit." If a certain step or thing is "according to the flesh," then you fall under the law of sin and death; but if you act according to the Spirit, then the "spirit" will be "life" because of righteousness—*i.e.*, obeying God and doing right.

In the conflict with the powers of darkness, we must understand that they are all around us in the air, *working alongside with* the "law of sin and death." When you obey that law of sin, you obey what the devil has brought into the world, and immediately you obey that law, the forces of Satan come upon you and push you down.

The Need of Watching

When you know this you will examine everything to see that you walk in all things according to the law of the Spirit, as far as you know how. It will make you watch. You will say, "I dare not walk according to the lower law any longer; I must walk according to the law of the Spirit of life."

We are given the pattern of this in Peter walking on the water. He walked step by step on the water, contrary to the law of gravitation, and would have continued walking if he had kept his eye on Christ. Such a simple thing as a "look" made him sink. Yes, simple; but it is in the simple little things that the enemy gains upon us. It is as long as you walk according to the Spirit of life in Christ Jesus that the Spirit of life will keep you from being controlled and dominated by the law of sin in your members.

Chapter 6

The Spirit of Him That Raised Up Jesus

*Not to Live After the Flesh—The Spirit of Adoption—
The Leading of the Spirit—Conformity to Christ*

LET us read Romans 8:11, "If the Spirit of *Him that raised up Jesus* from the dead. . . ." Note that the Lord Jesus did not raise Himself. He was raised from the dead by the Father. (See Rom. 6:4, Acts 2:24.) If the Spirit of the Father dwells in you, then, "He that raised up Christ Jesus from the dead *shall give life also to your mortal bodies through His Spirit* that dwelleth in you" (ASV). That quickening of the mortal body is practically the effect of verse 2 of the same chapter: "The law of the Spirit of life in Christ Jesus hath made me *free from the law of sin and*

death." One law is therefore set against another—
the law of sin and death versus the law of life in
Christ Jesus.

Suppose we make the truth more personal
and simple by reading verses 2 and 11 this way:
"The law of the Spirit in Christ Jesus makes me
free (v. 2), and if the Spirit of Him that raised
up Jesus from the dead dwells in me (v. 11), He
that raised up Christ Jesus from the dead shall
quicken my mortal body by His Spirit that dwells
in me."

The basis for all this life in Christ set forth
in the eighth of Romans follows *the fact of the
cross for the old creation* explained in the sixth of
Romans. I must repeat again: To know the life
described in the eighth of Romans we must
steadily stand on the footing of Romans 6:6,
"*knowing* this, that our old man was crucified
with Him" (ASV). Then, and only then, can we
know "the law of the Spirit of life in Christ Jesus"
making us "free from the law of sin and death."

Following the marvelous first eleven verses
of Romans 8, the apostle then points out the
obligation lying upon those who know all this.
"So then, brethren, we are *debtors*, not to the
flesh, to live after the flesh: for if ye live after the

flesh ye must die; but if by the Spirit ye put to death the deeds [margin, *doings*] of the body, ye shall live" (ASV).

Not to Live After the Flesh

The Spirit of life in Christ Jesus is dwelling in you. Therefore you are a "debtor" to God not to live after the flesh; for if you do, you will come under the law of death. You must by the same Spirit put to death—or cause to die—all the old doings of the body, and then you shall live. "For as many as are led by the Spirit of God, they are the sons of God"; *i.e.*, the "sons of God" walk after the Spirit, led by Him. And they are "sons" because they "received not the spirit of bondage," which brings fear, but they "received the Spirit of adoption," whereby they cry, "Abba, Father." "The Spirit Himself beareth witness with our spirit, that we are children of God" (v. 16, ASV).

Only by walking after the Spirit can we know the "leading of the Spirit," and only as many as are "led by the Spirit of God" are sons; *i.e.*, only in the spirit of sonship can any be led by the Spirit. It is not that they are led of the Spirit so as to *become* "sons." The fact that they are led by the Spirit of God is evidence that they *are* sons— and sonship means no bondage.

It takes the "Spirit of adoption" to enable us to cry "Father." We realize that God is a Father to us when we get to know the Father-spirit of the Father and the Son-spirit of the Son. In that knowledge we lose all terror and slavish fear of God and the sense of being in bondage to Him.

The Spirit of Adoption

The life after the Spirit is spontaneous and simple as the life of a child. It may be described as a divine-natural life. The Spirit of adoption produces in each believer the spirit of a child, the spirit of a son. The believer then knows God as Father—and who is afraid of a God-Father? One evidence that you are walking "after the Spirit" is that you have liberty in your spirit toward God, and you know Him as your Father.

But you say, "How am I to know this child-attitude to God?" This is the work of the Holy Spirit. "The Spirit *Himself!*"—He is a Person—

"beareth witness *with our spirit*, that we are children of God" (ASV). Notice here the distinction between the Holy Spirit and your spirit. We are given the witness of the Holy Spirit to *our spirit* that we are God's own sons, or children. If we are His children, then we are "heirs, heirs of God." *All that God has belongs to us*! We become joint-heirs with Christ, "if so be that we suffer with Him, that we may be also glorified with Him" (v. 17, ASV).

When you are brought into this life of the Spirit, the more you live and walk in it the more you will have the marks of the life as described by Paul: the quickening, the emancipating, the adopting, the leading, the witnessing and the interceding of the Holy Spirit. The law of the Spirit of life in Christ Jesus runs along these pathways in the spirit-life of the believer, and the marks of that law of the Spirit of life will be seen in you. What He is in the greater measure as God, we become in the lesser as the outcome of His handiwork. He works in and upon us, that He may work in others. Let us trace His work in the believer in several special directions as shown in this chapter.

The Leading of the Spirit

First, you will know the *leading* of the Spirit. You will get to know how He leads. You will lose all fear and bondage, for nothing that puts you into bondage is of God—not even in seeking blessing. Whenever you find a crushing weight upon you, you may know it is not of the Holy Spirit. If you feel in bondage about anything, bound up as it were, remember that every trace of bondage should go out of your life and every trace of fear. God does not put on you a spirit of terror. He gives you only the spirit of a child with a Father—filial fear, not slavish fear—with the co-witness of the Spirit, that you are a child saying "Father!"

Second, as the outcome of that life in the Spirit, is the *intercession* of the Spirit, which brings you into a groaning of Spirit-born prayer for all saints, and then "we know that to them that love God, God worketh all things with them for good" (v. 28, ASV margin). As the result of the ceaseless intercession of the Spirit, God is working all things for good with every member of the Body of Christ.

Conformity to Christ

The third outcome of life in the Spirit is *conformity* to Christ: "For whom He foreknew, He also foreordained to be conformed to the image of His Son, that He might be the firstborn among many brethren" (v. 29, ASV). Here we are told, in brief, what the Holy Spirit is groaning for: He is in groaning intercession for the *saints*; and as a result all things are being worked together for good to every child of God, so that each one might be "conformed to the image" of the "firstborn" Son of God—to Jesus Christ.

Let us just settle down upon these wondrous words and say, "While I do not understand and cannot tell what these trials mean, and why this conflict is in my life, yet I do know the love of God. I do know that the Holy Spirit is making intercession in the Body of Christ for all the members of the Body, and that the Lord Jesus is making intercession on the throne."

The Lord Jesus Christ carries on the intercession in heaven and the Holy Spirit the intercession within the church. Christ is on the throne interceding, and the Holy Spirit is in the members and in the whole Body of Christ interceding. Through the double intercession of Christ in heaven and that of the Spirit, God is working together all things to conform His children to the image of His Son. The creation is groaning for the manifestation of the sons; the Holy Spirit is pleading for the same thing. Christ in heaven and the Spirit in the church are both interceding for this conformity to the image of Christ, so that in due time there shall be the manifestation of the sons of God.

Look next in verse 31 at the apostle's conclusions based upon all this wonderful unveiling of the purpose and workings of God by His Spirit and through His Son. "What then shall we say to these things? If God is for us, who is against us?" (ASV), i.e., if the Holy Spirit is thus pleading, if God is "for us" as members of the Body of Christ, if God is "working all things together" for us to conform us to the image of Christ, then how can there be anything really *against* us? "All things" *means* "all things"! Then nothing can injure us if God is for us.

> He that spared not His own Son, but delivered Him up for us all, how shall He not also with Him freely give us all things? Who shall lay anything to the charge of God's elect? It is *God* that justifieth; who is he that

condemneth? Shall Christ Jesus that *died*, yea rather, that was *raised* from the dead, who is at the right hand of God, who also maketh intercession for us? (vv. 32–34, ASV margin)

See how Paul turns from the unveiling of God's purpose, and from the working of the Spirit in the children of God, to such a wonderful picture of Christ on the throne. How he unveils the heart of God, showing that God is working out all things in the life of every child of God, so that he may be conformed to the image of Christ.

This "all things" may include tribulation, distress, persecution, famine, nakedness, peril— even the sword (see v. 35)—but only for our good! Even in circumstances such as these, the goal is our conformity to the image of Christ. Remember, "God spared not His Son. . . ." And He loves you.

May the Holy Spirit Himself make true to every reader of these words all that they mean in the highest purposes of God for each of His redeemed ones. Amen.

PUBLICATIONS

Fort Washington, PA 19034

This book is published by CLC Publications, an outreach of CLC Ministries International. The purpose of CLC is to make evangelical Christian literature available to all nations so that people may come to faith and maturity in the Lord Jesus Christ. We hope this book has been life changing and has enriched your walk with God through the work of the Holy Spirit. If you would like to know more about CLC, we invite you to visit our website:

www.clcusa.org

To know more about the remarkable story of the founding of CLC International we encourage you to read

LEAP OF FAITH

Norman Grubb

Paperback
Size 5¹/₄ x 8, Pages 248
ISBN: 978-0-87508-650-7
ISBN (*e-book*): 978-1-61958-055-8